F I N D I N G
J O Y

Living an A+ Life in a C- World

Love life! Emma Coles

F I N D I N G
J O Y

Living an A+ Life in a C- World

C A R R I E   C O P L E Y

Book Press™
publishing

Published in Des Moines, Iowa, by:

BookPress Publishing
P.O. Box 71532
Des Moines, IA 50325
www.BookPressPublishing.com

Publisher's Cataloging-in-Publication Data

Names: Copley, Carrie, author.
Title: Finding Joy : Living an A+ life in a C- world / Carrie Copley.
Description: Des Moines, IA: BookPress Publishing, 2017.
Identifiers: ISBN 978-0-9967616-4-2 | LCCN 2017953546
Subjects: LCSH Self-Actualization (Psychology). | Success--Psychological aspects. | Imagery (Psychology) | Visualization. | BISAC SELF-HELP / Personal Growth / Success | SELF-HELP / Personal Growth / Happiness |
Classification: LCC BF637.S8 C6585 2017 | DDC 158/.1--dc23

First Edition
Printed in the United States of America
10 9 8 7 6 5 4 3 2 1

*This book is dedicated to all of my family and friends
who have helped me discover who I am in Christ,
which ultimately has led me to finding my deepest joy.*

CONTENTS

ACKNOWLEDGEMENTS

I would first like to acknowledge my husband, Chad, who is my best friend and biggest fan. This book would not have happened without his love, patience, encouragement, and honest feedback.

I would like to acknowledge my parents, Arleigh and Sue Clemens, for their support not only with the book, but also throughout my life. Your love and support guided me through my darkest days. Your simple acts of listening, love, support, and believing in me led me to finding real joy and purpose in my life.

Thank you to my children, Stephanie, Zachary, Taylor, and William, for all your patience, love, support, and helping me write my story—which is really "our" story.

Special thanks to Cathy Clemens and Cami McColley for reading my very first draft of "Finding Joy" and providing me with encouragement and honest critique. Most of all, I thank you for your belief in me, which pushed me to believe that I really could publish my first book.

Thank you to BookPress Publishing, especially Anthony Paustian, for coaching me through this entire process and being available to me every step of the way.

Most of all, I'd like to thank God. Thank You for waking me up at 3:00 am to name the book and for making it all come together after that 'conversation.' You have strengthened me throughout the years and you are truly the reason why I strive every day to live a life full of joy.

This Can't Be Happening

Carolyn woke up dazed and confused, feeling like she had drunk too much the night before. She could hear sounds of summer outside her bedroom window. Her mind then slowly shifted to the sounds inside her house of children crying in the family room and the low, deep voice of their father, Ben, talking to them. Suddenly, the memory of last night flashed through her head, and she flew out of bed and ran to her children. There by the fireplace, Ben held the children by his side, announcing that he would be moving out that day. Not only would he be moving out, but moving out of town. Rage went through Carolyn as she remembered the previous night's conversation. They had come home from a friend's party around midnight, and Ben had been in a cranky mood all evening. As they prepared for bed, Ben had quietly informed her that he didn't love her anymore and that he would leaving in the morning. She tried to reason with him

and begged him to try counseling first, but he just stared at her with an ice-cold expression. The only thing he would discuss was how to tell the children. It all seemed so surreal. This couldn't be happening. Everyone always said that they had the ideal marriage, and this wasn't what was supposed to happen in ideal marriages!

Carolyn couldn't believe what she was hearing. She threw down a kitchen chair in a fit of anger and screamed, "This isn't how we agreed! What are you doing?" She tried to calm herself down. Her frightened children looked at their crazed mom and cried harder. Ben simply said, "I told them."

Carolyn wanted to punch him. She wanted to hug him. She wanted to beg him to stay, but all that came out were deep sobs of disbelief as she watched him take his belongings and leave. She knew she had to stay strong, but she didn't know how she was going to do it. She had married young and had never even been on her own. Now she was left alone, with three children who needed her more than ever, and she wondered where she would ever find the strength to give them everything they needed.

As the weeks passed, Carolyn became obsessed with trying to understand what happened to the man she loved and to whom she had been married to for over 15 years, her children's father. How could he just walk out and leave not only her, but his beautiful children. Over the weeks and months, she learned many things about Ben that she simply couldn't believe. It truly seemed that he had led a secret life. How could she have been so naïve? He had taken their money, created credit card accounts in her name, and told lies to his

family and friends about their marriage. Carolyn also learned that he had been involved in numerous affairs and had left for another woman he apparently met on the internet. All she could think was, *"there has to be mistake."* This crazy stuff couldn't be happening; this was the kind of story that gets aired on *Dr. Phil*! Friends and family reached out and helped as much as they knew how, but as she shared her story over and over, she only grew angrier. If sides had to be taken in the matter, everyone would have sided with her, except his parents. She thought that sharing her story would make her feel better, but in reality, she only felt worse. She felt like a victim.

The Conversation

Months passed, and although Carolyn managed to get into a new routine, she still struggled day to day. She was so angry. She had heard that time heals all wounds, but she knew in her heart that this pain was going to take years to heal. She didn't sleep well, tossing and turning through most of her nights. The story of her life ran through her head night after night as she tried to figure out where things went wrong. They probably didn't have a perfect marriage, but it had been good. She couldn't remember the last fight they had. In fact, she couldn't remember any fights between them.

Carolyn woke up early one day and decided to get a jump start on her day at work. It was harder for her to focus at work these days with so many of her own problems. Though she loved her job as an administrator at a children's residential treatment center, it had become taxing to her soul. She was going through her own personal crisis, yet every day

there seemed to be some sort of challenge with a child, family, or staff member requiring her attention. She was easily distracted when good-hearted co-workers asked how she was doing. She would stop and share the latest saga going on in her life, and she always received a lot of sympathy and hugs from her friends and co-workers.

Carolyn had just arrived to work and was checking her mail when Kim walked in. Kim was the CEO of the company and her office was at another site, so they didn't have a lot of interaction. Kim told Carolyn that she had heard of her difficulties and asked if she would be interested in grabbing lunch that afternoon, as she had something that she wanted to share with her. She wouldn't give her any more details and suggested that they meet back up at noon. The morning went by slowly for Carolyn. She kept wondering what Kim could want to share with her. Carolyn couldn't remember ever having a conversation with Kim except for business matters and the occasional, "Hi." She hoped lunch wouldn't be awkward!

Kim stopped by her office promptly at noon, and they drove to lunch. Carolyn was thankful that picking the restaurant was an easy process. For weeks after Ben left, all she could eat without getting an upset stomach were baby carrots and Diet Coke. This "diet" was great for weight loss, but she joked with her friends that she wouldn't recommend it to her worst enemy. After they sat down, Carolyn quickly decided on chicken strips with a side of fries. She loved being able to eat without having to worry about her weight. Kim started the conversation by asking Carolyn about her recent divorce,

which opened a floodgate of victim stories about what happened to her and her kids. Carolyn laughed as the food arrived and said, "Do you think if I write a book, Dr. Phil will have me on his show?"

Kim smiled. Carolyn was just getting ready to bite into a chicken strip when Kim said, "I'm sorry that all happened to you and your kids, but can I ask what part of this was your fault?" Carolyn couldn't believe it. Had Kim not heard the story? She felt her neck and face start to turn red. Her heart raced, and she wanted to cry. Everyone had been so kind to her and had agreed that it was all Ben's fault. How could Kim even suggest such a thing? The waiter stopped by to fill the water glasses and must have felt the tension at the table, because he quickly left.

When Carolyn could compose herself enough to talk, the only thing that she could muster was, "Excuse me, did you not hear my story? He walked out, he cheated, he took all the money, and he lied…Did you not hear me say that?" She could hear her voice becoming shaky and escalated. She had to remind herself that she was eating lunch with her CEO. She took a deep breath and fought back more tears, silently cursing herself for accepting this lunch date.

Kim put her hand on Carolyn's hand and with a kind, compassionate smile, said, "I did hear you, Carolyn, and I'm so sorry that your marriage ended that way, but that was the end. What happened in the beginning and the middle of your marriage to create such a mess? Carolyn, what did you ignore? What did you not address? What did you not deal with and stick your head in the sand?"

From deep down inside, the answers started to come to Carolyn. No one had asked her what she had done; in fact, she was so busy being angry and blaming all of the problems on Ben that it never occurred to her that she could have been part of the problem. Carolyn had so many emotions running through her head. Her stomach hurt again and she wanted to cry, but she didn't dare allow herself as she knew the tears wouldn't stop for a long time. Kim rubbed her hand and shared that many years ago, she had been through a very difficult journey and she too was filled with anger and bitterness. Carolyn couldn't imagine Kim full of anger and bitterness. Everyone knew her as a kind, compassionate person who by all appearances loved her life. As if Kim knew what Carolyn was thinking, she laughed. She asked Carolyn if she wanted to change how she felt about her life. That was easy for Carolyn, and she answered with a resounding yes.

Kim's next question caught her off her guard: "If I were to ask you to grade your life in all areas one year ago, what grade would you have given it?" Carolyn looked at Kim, not exactly sure what she was talking about. Kim noticed the look and laughed. "Carolyn, if an A equals awesome, B equals better than average, C equals okay, probably average, D equals down in the dumps and F equals flunking big time, what grade would you give yourself one year ago?"

Carolyn thought quickly about the previous year. Her initial instinct was to say a "C", but that sounded awful. If she said "C", that would mean average, just okay, not perfect, and certainly not wonderful. She already told everyone that her life had been great before this mess. Kim finished her salad

while the grades went through Carolyn's head. Then quietly Carolyn said, "C, only a C."

Kim nodded and said, "Are you willing to do the hard work and make your life an A, maybe even an A+?"

Carolyn couldn't imagine what that would look like, but she was tired of feeling horrible and tired of the negative energy wherever she went, so she eagerly said, "I don't have any idea what you are talking about, Kim, but yes, I'm ready."

Before lunch ended, Kim told Carolyn that many years ago, a friend helped her when her life wasn't going in the direction she wanted. The friend had agreed to share the six secrets of living an A+ life with her if she would consider sharing the six secrets with others who might benefit. She couldn't help but think that these simple six secrets would not only change Carolyn's life but also the lives of her children. She asked Carolyn if after she learned these secrets, she would open her heart and consider sharing them with others in her future, and Carolyn quickly agreed. She just wanted to get started. They agreed to have meetings once a week, during which Kim said Carolyn would be given "lifework" assignments to do. Kim shared that the word "homework" had too many negative connotations, so she simply created a new word: lifework. She said lifework involved fun, thought-provoking questions and assignments meant to dig into the real you.

They ended lunch with a hug. Carolyn couldn't believe it; the CEO of her company was going to help her change her life! As they started back to work, Kim said, "Oh, one more thing… before we meet again, I want you to write down what

an A+ life looks like to you. Ask yourself what you want your life to look like in the next five years. I want you to dream big! What do you want your relationships to look like? Where do you want to be living? What do you want to be doing for work? Don't worry, I won't be offended if it's not here!" She laughed and continued, "What do you want your finances to look like? What do you want your mental and physical health to look like?"

Carolyn laughed and said, "I'm getting overwhelmed just thinking about all these questions. How am I supposed to know what my life will look like next year, let alone in five years?"

Kim smiled and said, "Carolyn, this is your life. Don't waste your time writing about winning the lottery and taking exotic trips. Just be real. Write from your heart. Where would you love to see your life in five years?" Kim gave her a hug and said, "Before you can create an A+ life, you must first create a vision of what an A+ life means to you. To put it another way, Carolyn, before you can create greatness, you first must have a vision of what greatness means to you."

Carolyn hurried back to her office with Kim's questions whirling around in her head. All afternoon, their lunch conversation ran through her mind. The thought that she couldn't escape was: why hadn't her family or her friends asked her what part of her divorce was her responsibility? They had all heard her story a million times, and no one had asked her that question.

The Aha Moment

Carolyn was so distracted that night with picking up the kids, making dinner, and helping with homework that she thought very little about Kim's assignment. After the last child was safely tucked into bed, Carolyn decided it was time for a glass of wine and some deep personal reflection. But, this time would be different. She decided she must first answer Kim's question about what part of this whole mess was her fault.

It was probably best to start at the beginning instead of the end. She laughed, remembering meeting Ben at a college party. He was fun. Although he was only one year older than she was, he seemed older and more mature, and she liked that about him. They started dating, and the first few months were a lot of fun, maybe too much fun. She couldn't recall him ever studying and he often skipped classes, but who was she to judge? She never missed a class, but almost always fell

asleep during lectures. Unfortunately, the university and his parents didn't approve of his grades, and he was asked to take a break from college. Carolyn laughed at how she initially thought he was mature. Nothing mature about that behavior! She gave a big sigh as she thought about how naïve she had been. They had managed to see each other most weekends, and they talked of marriage. She wondered out loud, "Why on earth did I want to get married so young?"

She also recalled the weekend that he told her he had joined the Army. He would be leaving in a few months for basic training, and he hoped to be stationed in Germany. This vision for their life appeared to excite him. She could clearly remember feeling that this wasn't her vision, but she had smiled and accepted this as part of her future even though she couldn't imagine leaving her family. They were married within a year, and sure enough, he was stationed in Garlstedt, Germany. Carolyn shook her head in sadness. She remembered being sad and embarrassed, making excuses for him when asked by family and friends why he seldom wrote or called from overseas. She wondered why she did that.

Finances had always been an issue in their marriage. Ben loved to spend money and would often lie about what he bought. It never made sense to her, but he would apologize, and life would go on. She remembered the time she found the name of his female co-worker written all over a small notebook he used. She found it odd and asked him about it. She could only remember that she didn't believe his answer. At that time, they had been married four years. She was attending a university, working full time, and trying her

best to be a good wife and mom. She knew something wasn't right, but chose to ignore it.

Story after story went through Carolyn's head, and finally she whispered out loud, "I'm an ignorer." She wasn't sure that was a word, but she didn't care. Every time there was a struggle, she would put her head in the sand and ignore the problem, too busy living to deal with the little annoying things he did. Too busy living to address any of the issues, the lies, or the concerns. A tear rolled down her cheek as she thought, *I always ignored the bad or forgave his lies, yet he was the one who walked out.* She quietly vowed to herself that she would never again live her life that way, not with her children and maybe someday future husband, if she could ever open her heart again to trust and love. It was time for bed, and she smiled as she crawled under the covers thinking, *I know one thing that I want in my vision assignment. I never again want to ignore problems. I want all my relationships to be open and honest, loving and trusting.* She dreamed about that as she fell asleep.

The Best Question

Carolyn couldn't believe it. It was already Friday, and she hadn't even started to put together what her A+ life should look like. All she could think about was how her life used to be and how she had been so naïve in thinking that it had been a good life. She mumbled to herself that she must have had low standards. *No more,* she thought, *no more!* Carolyn pulled into the Applebee's parking lot where she was meeting her best friend, Ruth, for dinner. She was excited to catch up on Ruth's love life and to tell her what Kim had shared about envisioning an A+ life.

Carolyn spotted Ruth sitting in a booth in the back, and she laughed as she sat down. Her dear friend had already ordered her favorite red wine for her, cabernet sauvignon, and it was on the table waiting. Carolyn loved to hear about Ruth's dating life. She couldn't begin to think about dating; the thought of it turned her stomach sour. Ruth had been

dating a man for about a year. They loved to travel and be together, but neither one of them had any desire for anything different. Carolyn admired how their relationship worked, but shared with Ruth that she would never want a relationship without commitment. They had known each other for years and respected and loved each other, even if they didn't always agree with each other's choices.

Carolyn's chicken fajita roll-up came, and she had just taken her first bite when Ruth asked about her job. Carolyn was so excited to tell her about lunch with Kim that she opened her mouth to talk and food flew out. They laughed so hard that others in the restaurant turned to stare, which only made them laugh harder. She took a big gulp of water so that she could share everything with Ruth. At first, Ruth couldn't believe that the CEO of Carolyn's company would ask her such personal questions. "How dare she ask you what part was your fault!"

Carolyn could see that this question also hurt Ruth. She took Ruth's hand, looked her in the eye, and said, "At first I thought it was a hurtful question, but it was probably one of the best questions I've been asked throughout this whole mess. In fact, it's probably a game-changing question for me."

Ruth shook her head, not understanding. Carolyn went on, "You, me, my parents, family, friends—we all blamed Ben. I'm not saying that he isn't at fault, especially considering how he handled it all, but the real question is why I was blind-sided. What was going on with me that made me unaware? What part of a broken marriage did I need to own?"

Ruth nodded and asked, "Well, did you figure it out?"

Carolyn sighed. "I went through 17 years of dating and marriage as an ignorer."

Ruth laughed. "A what?"

Carolyn shared how she spent the other night reflecting on all the years she had been with Ben, how she was a conflict-avoider and a stick-your-head-in-the-sand kind of gal. "Forgive, forget, and move on must have been buried in my subconscious. No wonder we seldom had a fight. I ignored the problems because I didn't like to fight, and it blew up in my face. Now I'm fighting to create a new life, a new me. I've made a vow to myself to never again bury my head in the sand. I want all my relationships to be open and honest, loving and trusting."

Ruth smiled and said, "You go girl!"

Carolyn laughed and told her about Kim's promise to teach her the six secrets of living an A+ life. Ruth said she wanted to hear more, obviously interested in how to live an A+ life. Carolyn said, "Kim wants me to create a life vision plan, or an LVP, of what I want my life to look like in five years. She compared a life vision plan to a business plan, but for life. To be honest, Ruth, I just don't know what that means yet. How am I supposed to know what my life will look like in five years? I'm just trying to survive each day!"

Ruth smiled and said, "I think we need another glass of wine, because I think I just identified your thinking error!"

"My what?" asked Carolyn.

"Carolyn," Ruth said, "Let me honest with you. Kim is encouraging you to dream big about what you want your life

to look like, right? The problem is, instead of dreaming big, you are staying stuck in today's problems and focusing on your troubles today instead of thinking about what you want your life to look like. In an ideal world, what would you want your life to look like? Do you want to be married again? I know that you are not 100% crazy about your job. Do you still want to be working there in five years? What kind of relationships do you want with your kids? The stress has caused you to lose a lot of weight this year, but what else do you want your physical and mental health to look like? What are you going to do for fun and creativity, and, lastly, am I still going to be your best friend?" Ruth took a big drink of her wine and went on. "Carolyn, my friend, you are not a victim. You can be the hero of your own life. A business plan helps you run and plan your business with focus and intention, right? If it is important to have a business plan for success, doesn't it just make sense for all of us to have an LVP? Think about it. To create a life you love, you must be intentional. To be intentional, you must know what you are shooting for, thus the need for an LVP. Doesn't this just make sense?"

Carolyn sat quietly and let all this sink in. She knew in her heart just what she needed to do this weekend, and she couldn't wait to share her plan with Ruth, Kim, and even her family. Carolyn smiled at her friend and told her she couldn't wait to get started.

Mind Dump

The house was quiet when Carolyn got home. She remembered how she would spend her whole weekend crying when the kids had a weekend at their dad's, but now she found herself enjoying her time alone. She put on her favorite pajamas and crawled into bed with an old notebook to get her life vision plan started.

She had experienced a light bulb moment talking to Ruth at dinner, and she knew exactly how she wanted to create her life vision plan. She was a business woman, and she knew the reason her company was so successful was because of its business plan. All department heads were held accountable to the plan, and they reviewed it quarterly to help guide the company to a larger vision. Carolyn couldn't believe that she never had this thought before, but it was in her blood now, and she was going to create her very own business plan—her very own life vison plan. Carolyn decided

to start writing whatever came to her. Things she hadn't thought about for years started to flow into her memory, and she wrote and wrote. She felt so alive as she started to dream about different ideas and thoughts of how she wanted her life to look in the next five-plus years.

She laughed as she read over all she had written and said out loud, "That certainly was a mind dump!" She glanced at the clock and couldn't believe that it was 1:15 in the morning. She decided that a good life plan would be best created with a refreshed mind, so she turned out the light, excited to begin work the following day.

The following morning, Carolyn awoke to the warm sun shining in her bedroom window. She glanced at the clock and was surprised to see it was already 9:15 am. She was always out of bed before the sun rose, but she had to admit that it felt good to sleep in. She pulled on her robe and walked into the kitchen to have her first cup of coffee. She had loved Saturday mornings when they were all there, *back in the good old days,* she thought. The kids would cuddle together on the couch to watch their favorite cartoons, and she would watch Ben cook a delicious breakfast while she sipped her freshly brewed coffee. Breakfast had been one of her favorite meals, but not now. She opened the cupboard and pulled out a box of Grape-Nuts, currently part of her healthcare plan. She searched the refrigerator for blueberries and silently cursed herself for forgetting to buy them the other night. As she slowly ate her cereal, she reviewed her notes from the night before and smiled, trying to read her horrible handwriting. She could feel the warm sun on her

back, and she decided to throw on some old clothes and head to the Ledges State Park in Boone to start creating her life vision plan.

6

Monday

Carolyn felt so alive as she pulled into the office Monday morning. Spending time in nature and walking the trails at the Ledges State Park had been just what she needed to refocus. She was tired of feeling depressed and bitter and was determined to start living and creating her "new normal." She made a vow to herself while walking the trails that her new normal would be a life filled with peace and joy. She smiled as she sat down at her desk and wished that her lunch with Kim was today, as she was excited to share her plan. Ruth had stopped by on Sunday afternoon, but Carolyn did not share it with her at that time. She kept having this recurring thought: *What if I can't create the vision I planned? What if I fail? What if this is a waste of time?* By evening, she had shaken off most of those feelings and almost called Ruth to come over to read it. But, the kids were coming home soon, and she wanted to be able to focus on them

instead of spending more time thinking about herself. She smiled as she thought that her time alone was truly the only blessing of the divorce.

The day went by quickly, as most of her days did. She never seemed to have enough time to accomplish everything she wanted to do. She wondered if that was something she should think more about. *Why don't I have enough time? Maybe if I worked more and talked less about my issues, I'd get a whole lot more done.* She decided she probably shouldn't share that thought with Kim!

Carolyn hurried home after work. The girls had soccer, and she hadn't even thought about dinner. She had sworn that she was going to make something at home instead of getting drive-thru fast food. The kids had started to complain about going out to eat. She promised herself that she would start making a weekly menu again. That had worked out so well before, and she wondered how she had forgotten all about that simple idea that made all their lives easier. She was relieved to find enough leftover spaghetti and wilted salad to feed them all. The meal didn't do much for her, but her kids finished all the leftovers, and they all agreed that it was better than fast food. Carolyn promised herself that after dinner, soccer practice, homework help, and bedtime routines, she would read through her life vision plan one more time before she shared it with Kim tomorrow at lunch. She was so excited that she didn't know if she would be able to sleep.

7

The Secrets Begin

Carolyn's stomach was turning. The night before, she had been so excited she could hardly sleep, and now she felt like she might throw up. What if Kim said she did her life vision plan wrong, or worse yet, what if Kim thought it was stupid? She glanced at the clock. It was 10:34 am. She was meeting Kim in less than an hour. She was filled with self-doubt and worry and wondered if she should just cancel the meeting and tell her CEO thank you, but no thanks. *Kim, thanks for lunch last week. I had a lot of fun working on my LVP, but now I'm terrified about what you might think, so let's just call it quits so neither of us has to feel embarrassed.* She hated when her brain filled her with self-doubt, and she wondered why on Earth she was thinking about sabotaging this opportunity.

Her phone dinged at that exact moment, and she looked down to see that Kim had sent her a text. *See you in 40*

minutes. I can't wait to hear what you created! She even added a smiling Emoji. Carolyn responded with a thumbs-up, which took all the courage she had at the moment. She decided she was going no matter what.

Carolyn walked slowly down the hall toward the parking lot, trying to give herself a pep talk. She wondered if Kim had been afraid to share her vision with her mentor, and why she felt afraid. She had been so excited to share her vision she could hardly sleep, and now she was terrified to share it with the one person who was trying to help her.

Carolyn noticed Kim's cute red sports car pulling into the parking lot and hurried out to greet her. She hopped in and closed the door as Kim looked at her, smiled, and asked her if it had been hard to come today? Carolyn couldn't believe Kim had just said that. She felt a wave of relief instantly wash over her. "YES," she said, maybe a little too loud, and then laughed and said, "How did you know?" Kim said she remembered when it was time to share her vision with her mentor, and that she had gotten so nervous she had thrown up and almost quit. She shared that she couldn't figure out how to quit, so she went and was so thankful that she hadn't let a little vomit hold her back. She laughed, saying that this memory had popped into her head this morning, making her decide to text Carolyn, just in case she had some anxiety. Carolyn confessed that she too had some self-doubt and hadn't known how to call and tell Kim she quit. She laughed and said, "I just don't understand why I almost talked myself out of coming and sharing." Kim looked at her and smiled, because she knew that Carolyn would find

out that answer in the coming weeks.

Kim pulled into the parking lot of Irish Bay's. Carolyn was excited about Kim's choice for lunch, as she had been wanting to eat there and knew her kids would never pick this type of restaurant. Kim said, "I hope that this is okay. I want you to meet someone." Carolyn secretly hoped that this "meeting someone" didn't use up very much of their time.

The server seemed to be expecting them and seated them quickly. Kim told Carolyn that this had recently become one of her favorite places. She quickly chose Shepherd's Pie from the menu. Carolyn's stomach started to turn, and she wasn't sure if it was from being nervous or from being starved. She decided to play it safe and order a Reuben with fries. Their drinks came out shortly afterward, and then Kim stood up and gave the server a big hug. She then turned to introduce Stacie to Carolyn. Kim shared that Stacie had been her coach and mentor through the six secrets of living an A+ life ten years earlier, and she was forever grateful that Stacie had opened her mind and heart to a new way of living. Carolyn thought she noticed a tear rolling down Kim's cheek, but she tried not to stare. Kim shared that she had met Stacie when she had frequented another of Stacie's restaurants. Stacie had noticed Kim's sadness every time she came in, and one slow afternoon, she took the time to hear her story. Lo and behold, Kim's life changed.

Carolyn felt slightly embarrassed for assuming Stacie was just a server, not the owner. The restaurant was starting to get busy, and Stacie said that she wouldn't take up any more of their time. Before she returned to work, she gave

Carolyn a warm hug and said, "I promise, if you do the work, even your biggest dream can come true. My dream did, and now I get to live it every day." She walked off with a huge grin to seat the next customer. Carolyn looked at Kim and said, "Let me guess, her big dream was to open this restaurant?"

Kim smiled and said, "You're thinking too small, Carolyn my dear. Part of her life vision plan was to open a chain of restaurants, and this is her third… and she still loves coming into work every day and loves what she does!"

The food arrived, nice and hot. Carolyn took the first bite, and it was as delicious as she imagined. She was still chewing when Kim said, "Enough of this small talk. We need to get to you and what you want your life vision plan to look like." Carolyn was thankful that her mouth was full of food, which gave her a few seconds more before she made herself vulnerable by sharing her vision. She took a gulp of water and started, "My life vision…" She briefly stopped and gave Kim a nervous smile, then looked down and read:

"I intend to have wonderful relationships with all of my family. I have found someone special to spend my life with, and we have a strong marriage and enjoy spending time together. We have positive, uplifting, nurturing, loving relationships with our children that will continue to grow stronger into their adult lives. We love spending time together and having fun, and we feel free to share our hopes, dreams, and worries with one another.

"I intend to have a healthy body and mind by exercising them both daily. I am enjoying learning new things

and challenging myself daily through personal development. I love to be active, running, walking, swimming, etc. I have never been happier with my body and my weight.

"I intend to be financially secure and to be able to bless others financially. I intend to have a thriving business of my own which impacts people's lives, and I feel blessed that I love going to work every day and I am making a difference.

"I intend to honor God by living a life of joy, peace, and love in everything I do."

It felt good to have said it, but her heart raced as she dared to look at Kim for her response. Kim smiled and said, "Perfect!" A wave of relief washed over Carolyn as Kim went on to give her positive comments about her vision and how she had thought about so many areas of her life. Kim asked more questions about her vision, which made Carolyn dive deeper in order to answer. It felt good. For the first time in a long time, Carolyn felt empowered to truly live the life she desired.

Kim had just finished paying the bill when she looked at Carolyn with a smile, and said, "Carolyn, congratulations, you have just completed Secret #1."

A+ Life Secret #1

Before you can start living an A+ life,
you must first visualize your A+ life.

Kim went on, "This secret is the foundation of all the secrets." To find success in your life or even a goal, you must first define what success means to you. I want you to read

your life vision plan daily, and let it sink deep within your soul. Not only do I want you to read it, Carolyn, I want you to believe that you can make it happen."

As they got into the car, Carolyn glanced at the clock and was glad that she had been to lunch with Kim, because this had been a longer-than-average lunch hour. She had an appointment in twenty minutes, and she hoped that Kim hit all the traffic lights just right so she would have extra time before the meeting. As luck would have it, they hit every stoplight on the way back to the office. Carolyn started to get anxious at the first red light and a little more anxious at the second one in a row. Kim looked at her, smiled, and asked her if she was ready for her next assignments. Carolyn secretly hoped that this one would be a little easier, but then something clicked, and she said, "Assignments as in more than one?" At another red light, Kim turned to her and said, "The first assignment is to share this vision with people you trust and people who will encourage you on your journey."

Carolyn relaxed as she thought about sharing her vision with Ruth, her sister, and her parents. She was still debating in her head who else she should tell when Kim asked if she was ready for part two. She took a deep breath and said, "Ready!"

They were only about a block from the office when Kim said, "This one is a little deeper, and I want you to feel free to call me if you need extra help, okay?" Carolyn nodded. Kim went on, "The next thing you must do is figure out why you want this life vision plan to come true." She pulled into the parking lot and said, "Carolyn, people always

initially answer this question with a surface answer, not the real, deep-down honest answer. You must dig deep into your soul for this one."

Carolyn must have looked puzzled because Kim added, "Think of an onion, Carolyn. It has many layers, right? Peel off the top layer and you have a surface answer. Peel off the next layer and you are getting closer. Once you peel off all the layers, you will have your core WHY. Your core WHY is the real reason you want this vision." Carolyn was still puzzled, but Kim went on, "Think about the company's business plan for a minute. We plan for the future of the business, and we create goals and strategies to get there, but all of that must be in alignment with our purpose, or should I say our mission statement. Your WHY is like your very own mission statement. Remember to have fun with this, Carolyn. Dig deep, but have fun and enjoy the process."

The Layers of an Onion

Carolyn's afternoon at work flew by, and as she was leaving, she tried to remember Kim's two lifework assignments. She was thoroughly frustrated with herself and felt like an idiot for forgetting. She made a note to herself to remember to call Kim the following day to help her with her memory. She wondered if Kim would think it was weird if she took notes. She would also have to remember to ask her that question.

The kids were outside playing when she pulled into the sitter's driveway. She loved watching them play, especially when they didn't know she was watching them. Lisa had been so supportive of her and the kids throughout this past year. She was grateful for all of her help and the extra hours she watched the kids when needed. She got out of her car, and the kids ran toward her to give her big hugs. She made small talk with Lisa, and then they all hopped in the car to start their

evening. Carolyn wasn't feeling very hungry after her big lunch with Kim, but she knew the kids would be starved. Once again, she vowed silently to herself that she would start planning their weekly meals on Sunday instead of flying by the seat of her pants each night. She did a quick inventory in her head of food she had at home and decided that tonight they would have fish sticks for dinner.

She was thankful that no one had an evening activity that night and after searching the backpacks, it appeared that homework time would be easy breezy, meaning she didn't need to help anyone with math homework. She loved dinner time when they weren't in a rush, shoveling dinner down their throats so that they could get to practice or some other scheduled activity. When they weren't in a rush, everyone had time to talk about their day and what part they liked best. She loved hearing what they were learning and what was going on with their friendships. Secretly she wished that everyday life didn't have to be so full.

She was glad she could crawl into bed by 9:00 pm and have some time by herself before going to sleep. She pulled out her iPad and quickly glanced at Facebook. She smiled at some of the funny things in her newsfeed and even gave her sister a smiling Emoji on one of her posts. She sighed and wondered why everyone else's life looked a whole lot better than hers. In her heart, she knew that wasn't true, but she suddenly felt an overwhelming sadness. She hated that her kids were growing up in a "broken home" and that her marriage had become a statistic. This wasn't the life that she had wanted or planned, but it was a life she had somehow

helped to create.

Carolyn declared out loud, "Enough of this whiny thinking! It is what it is…now deal with it!" She decided to check her work email to get her mind off of her personal life and noticed that she had an email from Kim. She clicked on it and read: *Carolyn, I remember how overwhelmed I felt after I would have lunch with my mentor and I would kick myself that I hadn't taken notes. Just in case you are having some of the same feelings, I want to tell you that I love your life vision plan, or your LVP as we call it, and I can't wait to help you build systems to create the life you dream! Remember this week to share your LVP with people you trust and to work on creating your WHY statement. Don't forget to peel that "onion" all the way to the core.*

Carolyn felt a sense of relief wash over her, and sent a quick thank you back to Kim for sending the reminder. She decided against telling her that she couldn't remember what she was supposed to do—she felt so dumb for forgetting. She glanced at the clock and decided it was too late to call anyone to share her life vision plan, and instead decided to think about her big WHY. She found a piece of paper and quickly drew an onion on it. She laughed at her artwork, knowing without a doubt that art was not one of her gifts. She also knew that she was a visualizer, and she needed that silly picture of an onion to get herself thinking. She wrote down words that came to her as she reflected on her WHY. She looked at all the words she had written, and the overriding themes were faith, love, family, and money. That seemed easy. Could she have come up with her WHY too quickly? It

seemed like an honest WHY to her, but she decided as she
turned out the light that she should look at it again before her
next lunch with Kim.

The week flew by quickly. *Maybe too quickly,*
Carolyn thought. She decided to share her five-year LVP
with Ruth first. Ruth had been very excited for her and had
asked her lots of questions…even challenged her thinking.
That is what she enjoyed about their relationship. In fact,
her challenging questions had helped Carolyn dig a little
deeper and, perhaps, peel off a few more layers from the
onion to get closer to her core WHY. She was thankful that
she had a few more days to figure that one out. Her parents
were another story. She had called her parents that afternoon, as they always talked on Sunday. She loved how they
always put her on speaker phone while they talked to her
and each other. They listened as she shared her recent
conversation with Kim and her challenge to create a five-
year life vision plan. Their questions were simple, and they
ended with, "If it makes you happy, Carolyn, then we are
happy for you." Carolyn didn't know why the conversation
frustrated her, because she had known this was how they
were going to respond. Her parents were great encouragers,
but did they really understand who she was and who she
wanted to become?

She left messages for her sister, but hadn't shared with
her yet. Her sister lived in the same town as her parents,
and Carolyn figured her parents would probably share her
life vison plan with her sister before she had a chance. She
almost called her parents back to ask them not to, but then

decided, *What the heck? What does it matter?* She knew her sister would love this whole idea. *Who knows,* she thought, *maybe I should practice mentoring my sister through the six steps to an A+ life.*

The WHY

Carolyn decided to pull out her WHY statement one more time before she had lunch with Kim to review it. She smiled as she reflected on her initial thoughts about her WHY statement. She had spent each evening after the kids had gone to bed breaking down the words that had resonated with her from the first night: faith, love, family, health, and money.

She started with faith and reflected on her faith journey. She was frustrated with herself that her faith had gotten bumped to such a low priority in her life. Ever since her life fell apart, she had felt a gnawing in the pit of her stomach that she needed to explore and grow in her faith, but she had been slow to follow through. As she was reflecting, it suddenly occurred to her that she had stopped putting God first in her life. In fact, God wasn't even in second, third, or fourth place. In the busyness of life, she had just taken Him

for granted and usually only sought Him out during life's trials. She had been taught these lessons in her youth but had never done a good job of living her life this way. In her heart, she knew that this was a must and made a note to herself to revise her life vision plan. As she jotted down the note, a strange sense of happiness overcame her. She knew in her heart that she was on the right track…finally.

Carolyn looked at her five words again: faith, love, family, health, and money. She decided to put love and family together as she felt that they were one and the same. Her five-year vision was all about building strong relationships with her family. In fact, she had written in her LVP that she intended to have positive, uplifting, nurturing relationships with her kids. She not only intended to have these relationships in the next five years, but envisioned maintaining these strong relationships into their adulthood. She envisioned they would enjoy time with each other, not because they had to, but because they had fun together. She laughed, realizing that love and family had come together quite easily. Carolyn knew in her heart that she would have to be very intentional with this big vision. She could think of several times in her life that she said her family was a top priority. But in reality, her work all-too-often got bumped to the top. She struggled over whether to include the thought of a romantic relationship or even marriage while working on her vision but, in the end, she decided that was important to her. She also knew she would have to be very careful who she invited into her life because of the kids.

Carolyn laughed as she thought about the next word:

health. Just last year, she had complained to her doctor about gaining weight and having a more difficult time losing it. When her doctor asked what she did to take care of herself, she had laughed and said, "My current health plan consists of drinking red wine, eating dark chocolate, and always making sure that I have blueberries on my cereal." Her doctor did not think it was quite as funny. He suggested that she start a regular exercise plan because, at her age, the weight was going to come off more slowly. She had always been blessed with her health, and weight had never been an issue before. She reflected on her LVP and knew in her heart it was time to make her health a priority. She would be turning 37 at her next birthday, and her kids needed her to be around for a long time.

Finances initially made her feel a little guilty, and she pondered what that meant. She wanted to be able to provide for her family and, as a single parent, she already felt the strain on their family budget. She put in her life vision statement that her ultimate goal was to become an entrepreneur, as she could then be more in control of her income potential and have a more flexible schedule to be able to attend the kids' events. These events seemed to be scheduled all too often during work hours. Kim had told her to dream big in her life vision plan, so she did! She knew this was a big dream, because she needed her entire paycheck to cover her bills, but it was in her heart, so she had to put it down.

She thought about her parents' finances and how they had been there for her financially when Ben had left her with nothing in the bank and a car with 161,000 miles on it in need

of new tires before the winter. Her dad had recently decided to get all of the car's issues repaired so she could travel safely. Her parents had insisted that it was a gift and wouldn't let her pay them back. They had always been selfless with their money. They made a decent income, yet they lived simply. Growing up, she sometimes felt poor compared to some of her friends who seemed to always have the latest fashions and gadgets. She wasn't sure what she would have done without her parents' help. She had written in her LVP that this was a gift that she wanted to be able to give to her children and to others in need. Right now, she was practically living paycheck to paycheck, and you can't bless anyone financially living that way. She vowed to herself that this would change. In her heart, she knew that she needed to get control of her finances and learn to live a more disciplined life.

She glanced over the notes she had written to try to summarize her WHY statement when suddenly it hit her. In the quietness of her house, she tested it out loud: "To create a life where taking care of my faith, family, and health are my priorities." She liked it, but it still felt like something was missing. She tested some others out aloud and finally decided on: **"To be constantly striving to be the best version of myself with my family, health, and career and to honor God in all I do."** She shook her head, wondering where the heck that statement came from, as it certainly wasn't the path she was initially taking. Yet, there was something about it that she liked, and it seemed to fit. Carolyn pulled out her five-year life vision plan and re-read

it. Her plan stated that she would be active: running, walking, and eating healthier, and that she would love her body and weight. *Okay,* she thought, *That intention is covered.* Carolyn noted that her desire to have positive and uplifting relationships with her family were covered and that her career was covered. Whether she was an employee or the owner of her own company, she felt strongly that she should always strive to give her best. She re-read her WHY statement and loved how she ended it with honoring God in all she did. She smiled as she realized that her WHY statement was pretty much summed up with the last sentence in her LVP. The only thing that was missing was money. Her initial thought with money had been to make a lot of it. She thought, *Money is important, but I don't want to live a life where money is my driver.* In the end, she decided that money would be covered under her career and that her career would make enough money so she could bless her family and others when they needed help, just like her parents had done.

Carolyn was exhausted when she looked at the clock and saw that it was almost 11:00 pm. She had meant to just glance at her WHY statement, but she had ended up reflecting on it for about two hours, making sure that it was just right for Kim. She turned off the light and was trying to find a comfortable position to sleep when, suddenly, she asked herself out loud, "Why on Earth did I just say that I'm trying to make this silly WHY statement *right for Kim?*" She sat upright and turned the light back on so she could read her life vision plan and her WHY statement one

more time, making sure that it was right on target for her and her only. She closed her eyes and prayed that God would help her live the life she was envisioning for herself and her children.

10

The WHY Thief

C arolyn was starting to love Tuesdays. Her mornings were always full of meetings, which she used to dread. But, now she saw them as a blessing. A full schedule meant that she didn't have much time to think about herself before her lunch appointment with Kim. She walked into her last meeting of the morning and noticed that she had gotten a text from Kim. Kim had a meeting at 1:00 pm in the office, and she wondered if it would be okay to just order Jimmy John's so their meeting wouldn't need to be cut short. Carolyn loved Jimmy John's, probably a little bit too much. She sent Kim a quick text with her order. Her stomach growled as the meeting started.

Carolyn was walking toward her office when suddenly the thought occurred to her that Kim might not be religious at all, and she might think her WHY statement was foolish. Carolyn sat down and took a couple of deep breaths to get

herself focused and to remind herself that this wasn't about Kim. This was her WHY statement, and it had meaning to her, but she secretly hoped Kim wouldn't think it was stupid. Kim walked in and laughed, saying that Carolyn looked like she was in deep thought. Carolyn broke into a smile and confessed that she was nervous to share. Kim smiled back and said, "Well, let's just get it out in the open and have you share."

Carolyn took a deep breath and repeated her WHY statement by heart, **"To be constantly striving to be the best version of myself with my family, health, and career and to honor God in all I do."** There, she had said it out loud, and it felt good. Kim didn't laugh or tell her it was stupid, and instead asked a lot of meaningful questions. Her last question was why she had been so nervous to share. Carolyn was initially embarrassed, but found herself taking another deep breath and sharing that she wasn't sure what Kim's beliefs were or if she would think Carolyn was some kind of religious freak. Kim said it was one of the boldest WHY statements she had heard and reminded her, "It doesn't matter what anyone else thinks as it belongs to you and only you!" Kim went on, "Now that you have your LVP and WHY statement prepared, I want you to read them a minimum of three times each day until it becomes a part of who you are and what you believe. The best advice that was given to me, Carolyn, was to write up my WHY statement and place it where I spent a lot of time, like my office, my car, my kitchen, and even on my bathroom mirror, as reminders throughout my day. Your WHY statement is going to help you stay

focused even when you want to give up. It is your secret weapon to finding the success you desire. Carolyn, the better you know it and live it, the more likely you are to achieve and maintain it."

A+ Life Secret #2

Your WHY statement is your secret weapon to help you stay focused, even when you want to give up.

Carolyn wasn't the most creative person in the world, but she was excited to start putting up her WHY signs at home and in the car. She struggled briefly over whether to put signs up at work and then thought she might put a small WHY statement beside her desk and maybe one on her iPhone. Her mind drifted with the warm sun beaming in, and she was thinking about all the places where she could put her WHY statement when she heard Kim say, "Are you ready for what's next?"

Carolyn was embarrassed that she'd been caught spacing out and quickly apologized. Kim laughed and told her to quit being so embarrassed and apologetic for every-thing. Carolyn just smiled and said, "Ready." Kim glanced at the clock, saying she wished that they had more time to discuss the next thing Carolyn had to wrap her head around. She went on to say, "This next secret is about something that is often one of the biggest joy-killers out there. It can rob people of their dreams and make them lose their WHY if they aren't careful." Now she had Carolyn's attention, and whatever she was going to say, Carolyn was sure that she

needed to learn every detail, as she hadn't felt real joy in her life in forever.

Kim leaned forward and said, "The next thing we are going to discuss is working on your Stinkin' Thinkin' and learning to make friends with your Inner Bully. Your Stinkin' Thinkin' and your Inner Bully are relatives who live inside your head! They are the voices that fill your head with negativity and self-doubt. I have a couple of questions for you to think about, Carolyn. Do you bury your head in the sand and ignore problems?"

Carolyn felt her hands growing clammy. She had just shared that thought with Ruth. She tried to refocus as she heard Kim say, "Do you focus blame on others, looking to point the finger at them instead of looking to see what you could have done?"

Carolyn smiled at Kim and confirmed that so far, Kim was pointing out issues already discovered recently. Kim nodded and went on, obviously seeing this conversation was making Carolyn uncomfortable. "Your Inner Bully is that part of you that puts you down, makes you question yourself, and in all actuality, lowers your self-esteem. Let me give some small examples. Have you ever heard yourself say, 'I'm too old to figure out this technology, look at all those wrinkles, I'm so old, I'm so ugly, I'm so fat, my jeans look horrible on me, I could never follow through with my BIG dreams because I'm too old to get started, I'm too stupid, I'm…'"

Carolyn interrupted her and said, "I get your point. I've said all those things, but doesn't everyone?"

Kim answered with another question. "Carolyn, would

you say any of those things to your best friend?"

Carolyn thought of her friendship with Ruth and how hurt Ruth would be if she ever said any of those things to her. *That is simply not how you talk to someone you love,* she thought. "Of course not!" said Carolyn.

Kim took her hand and asked, "If you wouldn't say those things to someone you love, why do you think it's okay to say them to yourself... about yourself? Honestly, Carolyn, you are probably right that most people talk to themselves that way, but you can't fix what you don't know is a problem. You now know that it is a problem, and if you don't get control of your Inner Bully, your LVP and your WHY are going to be a struggle. Do you ever wonder why so few people accomplish their goals? They say that only about 10% of people accomplish their goals, which means that 90% of people fail. Worse yet, they fail within the first month!"

Carolyn thought of all the goals she had tried to accomplish over the past few years. She couldn't think of one success other than losing an extra 20 pounds, but she couldn't give herself credit for that. Before she could ask her what the 10% were doing differently, Kim put down her Coke and said with a smile on her face, "Those who find victory with their goals have learned how to identify their Stinkin' Thinkin' and their Inner Bully and know how to tune them out. In other words, Carolyn, they shut them up quickly. They have learned how to identify their sneaky ways and to call them on their lies." Carolyn was intrigued. She could identify a lot of Inner Bully moments in her life, but it had never occurred to her that she could stop that senseless chatter going on in

her head. She had no idea those crazy, mean thoughts could be tuned out...why hadn't someone told her that before? Their time was running short. Kim handed her a piece of paper. Carolyn glanced at the heading and quietly read to herself, *Stinkin' Thinkin' Symptoms.* "Oh my gosh," Carolyn said, "There's a whole page of them!"

Kim glanced at the clock and wished she had more time with Carolyn that afternoon. She asked Carolyn to review all the *Stinkin' Thinkin' Symptoms* and identify which ones she felt were an issue in her life. Kim asked her to pay extra attention over the next week to her words and thoughts and to be mindful of the times she noticed her Stinkin' Thinkin' and Inner Bully playing mind games with her. Kim suggested to gently observe what she said to herself when she noticed a symptom or a mind game being played inside her head and to simply change it to something different...something nicer. Kim also suggested that if she found herself saying these negative, self-sabotaging statements out loud that she ask trusted friends and family to help her identify when she said them. She said that her family helped her have victory over her Inner Bully.

As Kim stood up to leave the office, she said, "One last thing, Carolyn. Some people find that if they give their Inner Bully a name, it empowers them to take control and tell that Bully to knock it off. It can make tackling this whole Inner Bully thing kind of fun." Before Carolyn could ask, she said, "I call my Inner Bully Hellga, spelled with two Ls!" Both women were laughing as they parted ways.

Stinkin' Thinkin'

Carolyn sat down at her desk and pulled the list of *Stinkin' Thinkin' Symptoms* out of her purse. She gave a heavy sigh as she began to review the list.

Eleven symptoms that show you may be struggling with Stinkin' Thinkin':

1. **Perfectionist:** This bully expects you do everything perfectly and makes it difficult for you to accept your work or yourself without criticism. She can cause problems at work and at home, as nothing is ever good enough.

2. **Scarcity Thoughts:** This bully lets you think that things are never going to get better. She wants you to think that you will never have enough knowledge, money, resources, or time.

3. **Blaming the Past:** You might be struggling with this

bully if you hear yourself say, "I've been down this road before and it didn't work out, so why even go there?" This bully keeps you stuck in the past so you can't have the future you want.

4. **Being Defensive:** This bully likes to jump to the conclusion that someone is judging her or thinking the worst of her. She has a tone in her voice of, "What do you mean?"

5. **Taking Things Personally:** This bully likes to twist things around to make her feel sorry for herself. Taking things personally typically feels like people are intentionally wronging her, and she will often give up on goals or relationships, feeling it is someone or something else's fault.

6. **Comparing Self to Others:** This bully compares herself to her peers in all areas of her life. She judges her home, income, clothing, children, etc. – always against others.

7. **Victim Mindset:** This bully is like the Taking Things Personally bully, but goes a step further. If you hear yourself blaming others instead of looking at yourself, you may struggle with Victim Mindset.

8. **Excuses:** This bully is rampant in most people's minds. She always has her finger pointing at someone or something else. "It's not my fault I didn't get the paper turned in; the internet went down." "It's not my fault I didn't exercise this week; the weather was too cold." "It's not my fault dinner isn't ready; my mom called."

9. **Name Caller:** This bully is a mean one who turns to name calling when frustrated or unhappy. "You are so stupid!" "You look like a fat pig in those jeans!" "I can't believe you can't figure out this computer problem again; you're such an idiot!"

10. **Complainer:** This bully struggles to take ownership and often sounds whiny. "It's the teacher's fault; she only gave us enough time to complete one assignment." "I did my part; it's not my fault the team didn't follow through."

11. **Ignorer:** This bully deflects problems by becoming the jokester or by burying her head in the sand and ignoring the issue altogether.

Wow, Carolyn thought, *I have a serious issue with my Stinkin' Thinkin' and my Inner Bully.* She quickly reviewed the list one more time and put an asterisk by the ones she felt applied to her. She remembered Kim's words from lunch: "You can't change what you don't acknowledge." She knew she was going to have to call in reinforcements to find victory in her thinking.

Carolyn was thankful that she had remembered to throw chicken in the crockpot before she left for work. Chicken and dumplings was a family favorite, and all that was left was to add the dumplings. The kids helped set the table while they listened to the radio and danced around the kitchen. Everyone was in a good mood and, once again, Carolyn was thankful that they didn't have much going on that evening. She had made the decision on her drive home

to share her thinking errors, as she was now referring to them, with her kids and Ruth. She knew they wouldn't let her get away with any of that Stinkin' Thinkin' and they would help her find victory over her Inner Bully, whom she was still trying to name. *Maybe the kids can help*, she thought as she put the pot of chicken and dumplings on the kitchen table.

The kids listened and laughed as she shared the new secret she had learned at lunch with Kim. Even though they were young, she enjoyed sharing this new adventure with them and prayed that some of it would sink into their thinking. Carolyn was delighted that the kids were excited to help her kick out her Inner Bully. They even wanted to "play" and share where they had Stinkin' Thinkin' issues. Dessert was typically served only at special meals, but Carolyn announced that cookies would be served if everyone agreed to help her come up with a name for her Inner Bully. The kids cheered, and Carolyn felt over-whelmed with love and gratitude for her family and their love and support. They didn't even care that the cookies were not homemade! Everyone had suggestions but, in the end, Carolyn decided to call her Inner Bully Lucy. She remembered watching Charlie Brown cartoons as a kid. Lucy was trying to appear as though she was helping Charlie Brown, but ultimately she set him up for failure and embar-rassment among his friends. Lucy was a bully who was always looking for recognition in the wrong way. Lucy. Yes, she liked the way that sounded! By the end of the evening, everyone had an Inner Bully nickname and had agreed to help each other find success.

Carolyn was getting ready for bed when she heard her phone ding. She glanced down and smiled as she read a text from Kim. *I wanted to share this quote with you that helps me daily to fight the good fight against Hellga. I hope that it motivates you to find victory over your Inner Bully!*

> *"It's not what you say out of your mouth that determines your life, it's what you whisper to yourself that has the most power."*
> –Robert Kiyosaki

Carolyn smiled as she read it, and quickly sent Kim back a text saying, *love it and thank you!*

12

Lucy

Carolyn woke up before her alarm went off and decided to get out of bed and start her day. She made her coffee and took a seat in her favorite chair in the sunroom. She loved it when she could pull herself out of bed early and have quiet time to herself. Watching the sun come up was always an extra blessing. She sipped her coffee as she reviewed her Stinkin' Thinkin' list so she could begin to tackle her Inner Bully, Lucy, who was living within her and driving her crazy. She laughed out loud and thought about their family dinner and all the crazy names they had come up with. She was smiling to herself when suddenly she thought, *Who am I kidding? I'll never find victory over Lucy. My Stinkin' Thinkin' is just too big!*

"Oh my gosh," Carolyn said out loud, "I just did it. Lucy just came out!" She quickly looked at her Stinkin' Thinkin' Symptoms list and noted she had just had a Scarcity

Thought. Carolyn tried to remember what Kim had said she needed to do when she caught herself in Stinkin' Thinkin'. She took a deep breath and changed her thought to, *I might have a lot of Stinkin' Thinkin' going on right now, but dear Ms. Lucy, I will have victory over you!* Carolyn couldn't believe how energized that made her feel, and all she did was reword a whiny, negative statement into something more empowering. She loved it! She glanced at the clock and decided it was time to jump in the shower before the rest of the gang got up. She felt inside that today was going to be a good day.

She had just finished getting ready when she heard the alarm clocks going off in the kids' room. The kids had initially hated the idea of setting their own alarm clocks, but she had insisted, and it had turned out to make everyone's mornings more peaceful. She no longer had to nag the kids out of bed. She would simply walk by their room and tell them each good morning, and remind them that breakfast would be served at 7 am. She went down to the kitchen to get out cereal bowls and put cereal boxes on the counter.

She grumped to herself that she was such an idiot for not remembering to pick up a new box of Cap'n Crunch the last time she was at the grocery store, then grumped some more that no one ever wrote anything on the grocery list except her. She was tired of always having to be the one to remember everything. She was searching the pantry for something else for breakfast when it suddenly occurred to her that Lucy was changing her mood from good to grouchy, and she had almost gotten away with it!

Carolyn pulled out an old box of Rice Krispies and sat down at the kitchen table to reflect on what had just happened. She had been pleased with herself for getting up early and getting her day off to a good start. No one had even talked to her yet, but her mood had shifted from good to grouchy. She thought about what Lucy had said to her and shook her head. She had called herself an idiot and then whined about her memory. Carolyn grabbed a piece of paper and wrote down, "I am not an idiot. I am a loving mom who simply forgot to pick up the kids' favorite breakfast cereal, which isn't a big deal in the scheme of things." When the kids apologized for something, Carolyn always had them ask for forgiveness. So, Carolyn said to herself, "Carolyn, do you forgive yourself for calling yourself names and for becoming whiny over Cap'n Crunch?" Carolyn laughed to herself and said, "Yes! I forgive me." Carolyn felt foolish talking to herself, but she knew that if she was going to conquer Lucy, she was going to have to get over that and quickly!

The rest of her morning was so busy that she completely forgot about Lucy, submerging herself in work. Carolyn glanced at the clock and couldn't believe that it was almost 1:00 pm and she hadn't even had lunch yet. She decided to grab her lunch and head outside to the picnic table to enjoy the warmth of the afternoon sun. As she ate, she thought about her day and couldn't think of a single incident where Lucy had popped in and tried to fill her head with Stinkin' Thinkin'. She wondered why Lucy seldom showed up at work and decided her days were too full to have any time for Lucy and her negativity! The only thing she had time

for at work was work! Just as she was getting ready to go back in, she glanced down at her phone and noticed Ruth had sent her a text earlier. "Darn it," said Carolyn, "I keep forgetting to call Ruth back. How could I be such an idiot?" Carolyn picked up her phone to text back and apologize, when it hit her like a ton of bricks. She had called herself an idiot for the second time that day. She wondered why on Earth she would talk to herself that way over a silly phone call. Carolyn drew in a deep breath and changed her sentence to, "Darn it, I forgot to call Ruth back. I need to text her and ask her to call me tonight during soccer practice." Carolyn laughed and continued, "And yes, Carolyn, I forgive you for allowing Lucy to talk to me like that." Carolyn sent Ruth a quick text message and hurried back to the office.

Carolyn worked later than she wanted to and hoped on the way to soccer that the kids would be okay with drive-thru fast food for dinner. She was frustrated at leaving late, but was proud of herself when she fought Lucy trying to break into her thoughts with some Stinkin' Thinkin'.

She was beginning to understand what all this "mindfulness" talk was about. She knew she had always had these thoughts in her head and that they weren't always nice, but never knew that she could tell them to stop. She wondered how many years she had been calling herself names, especially "idiot!" *It's funny*, she thought, *I would send the kids to their room for calling one another an idiot, and yet I call myself an idiot. Why do I say that?*

She was thankful that she had called Lisa before she left the office to tell her that she was running late and would

be swinging by to pick up the kids shortly. She waved to Lisa as she pulled into the driveway and was grateful to have such an awesome babysitter. Lisa had reassured Carolyn that she would have the kids ready to go, and when she pulled in, sure enough, the kids were outside with backpacks on and looks of frustration on their faces. The kids jumped in, and she had barely pulled out of the driveway when the arguing started. The kids were frustrated at her tardiness, they complained about soccer and homework, and wanted to know what was for dinner. They whined when she announced they would be picking something up quickly to eat on the way to practice. Carolyn tried to breathe deeply through their complaints, but she could feel her anger building when she pulled into McDonald's. She pulled into a parking spot closest to the entrance, turned in frustration to her children, and said in a voice that was a little too loud, "I'm sorry that I'm such a terrible mom, making you eat at McDonalds instead of cooking like all your friends' moms, but I'm not them. Excuse for me failing as a mother!"

She could feel the tears coming, which was not what she had intended. She felt tired and overwhelmed, then her oldest child said, "Um, Mom, I think Lucy just showed up... I think she's using Name Calling, Excuses, and Comparing Yourself." The kids were all looking at her, not sure what her response would be, as Carolyn sat there quietly. Suddenly, she gave a loud laugh. Her laughter broke the tension, and they all got out of the car giggling and hugging. Carolyn apologized for freaking out and asked her children to forgive her, which they eagerly did.

By Tuesday, Carolyn didn't know if she should be excited to meet with Kim or run screaming in the opposite direction. She was frustrated with herself and her numerous thinking errors, and she wondered if she could ever make Lucy her friend instead of her Inner Bully.

Kim must have seen the frustration on Carolyn's face when she pulled into the parking lot, because as Carolyn buckled up, she reached over and put her hand on her shoulder. "Let me guess," she said. "This Stinkin' Thinkin' assignment has been rough." Carolyn began to agree, but instead burst into tears. It had been hard enough getting the kids out the door on time that morning, but as soon as she came into work, she'd had to deal with complaints from both co-workers and clients. Carolyn shared through her tears that she was having the most trouble with Name Calling and Scarcity Thoughts, and she wondered if she could ever really change. Kim reached over and squeezed her hand. Carolyn grabbed a tissue and dabbed it under her eyes. She hated her mascara running down her face. Kim suggested they grab something to eat at a nearby drive-thru and then go to the park to eat. Carolyn knew that Kim was looking out for her. She needed time to pull herself together before she had to go back to work.

Kim gave Carolyn a big hug before they sat down to eat at the park. Carolyn asked her if it had been this difficult for her to change her thinking errors. Kim smiled and said, "Carolyn, I still have days where I battle Hellga, but the good news is that I'm much quicker to spot that type of thinking and to correct myself." As she sat down, she eased Carolyn's

worries about it never changing by reminding her that Lucy has been wreaking havoc in her thinking for years, and there was no overnight thinking error cure. "The good news is that you've identified Lucy, you've named the problem, and now the real work can begin of turning Lucy into your Inner Cheerleader." This made Carolyn smile. She liked the challenge of turning Lucy into her Inner Cheerleader!

They spent most of their lunch swapping Lucy and Hellga stories that made them both laugh. Kim laughed so hard her face turned red when Carolyn shared the story about her freaking out at McDonald's and being reminded by her daughter that Lucy had just joined them. Kim shared that Hellga wanted to join her on every errand and attempt to remind her what a horrible sense of direction she had. She added, "Unfortunately, my husband all too often agrees with Hellga, and I have to figure out how to tune them both out!"

Carolyn could feel the weight of her difficult morning lifting, and she was glad she hadn't run screaming in the opposite direction. Kim glanced at her watch. They had to wrap up soon. She asked Carolyn if she was ready for her next assignment. Carolyn hastily said, "Yes." Kim smiled as if she knew that this assignment had been frustrating at times for Carolyn, but also knew it wouldn't end just like that. "Before I share the next secret, let me say congratulations for sticking through this adventure with me for the past three weeks. Mastering your mindset and controlling your Inner Bully is a game-changer in your life. Learning how to identify your Stinkin' Thinkin' and changing your thoughts will not only help you love yourself in a deeper, more meaningful

way, but it will also help you accomplish your biggest goals and dreams."

A+ Life Secret #3

You must learn how to master your mindset and turn your Inner Bully into your Inner Cheerleader.

Kim gave Carolyn's hand a squeeze and said, "Carolyn, your friend Lucy is going to be with you for life, and Lucy isn't always nice. She often lives in fear and doubt. Your job is to identify when she is attacking you and to learn how to tune her out. This isn't an overnight process, but a lifelong challenge. Are you ready for this challenge?"

Carolyn laughed and said, "I'm always ready for a challenge…game on!"

They stood up to head back to the car, and Carolyn said, "Wait, what about secret number four?"

"Oh my gosh," Kim said, "I got so caught up with secret number three that I completely forgot about sharing the next secret. She glanced at her watch and asked Carolyn if she could spare an extra fifteen minutes so she could explain the next secret.

Carolyn laughed and said, "Only if you don't tell the boss that I'm late." They laughed as they sat back down at the picnic table to discuss the next lesson. Kim told Carolyn that this next assignment was very much like her previous Stinkin' Thinkin' assignment. In fact, they would complement each other. Carolyn smiled at Kim, but she wasn't feeling overly excited. She was tired of her thinking errors and wondered how she was ever going to fix herself. Kim

seemed to understand her anxiety and gave her a nod. "Carolyn, your next assignment is to think throughout your day of what you are grateful for and to journal daily a minimum of five to ten blessings in your life." Kim encouraged Carolyn to pick a time each day to do her journaling and to write something different each time.

Carolyn laughed and said, "That's it? This should be easy-peasy after this last week."

Kim just smiled as they walked back to the car.

Two for the Price of One

K im went on to say, "In life, we typically get what we focus on. If we focus on our problems, it seems we have more problems. Therefore, if we focus on blessings, we are apt to see blessings in our lives.

This made Carolyn laugh out loud. With her arms raised in the air, she said, "Why didn't someone tell me this months ago?" This made them both laugh.

"I wish someone would have, but just because you now have this information doesn't mean it is easy to make the switch in your thinking. This week and for the rest of your life, I want you to journal every day at least once a day about what you are grateful for." Carolyn sarcastically stated that this wouldn't take much time out of her daily schedule. Her reaction seemed to catch Kim slightly off guard. She looked Carolyn in the eye and said, "Carolyn, I want you to repeat after me, *"I'm too blessed to be stressed."*

Carolyn felt silly, but repeated *"I'm too blessed to be stressed."* Kim encouraged her to continue repeating the phrase until Carolyn's tone of voice became a little irritated. Kim picked up on her irritation and asked her to now start listing things in her life that she was grateful for. She asked her to continue to name things until she no longer felt stressed. Carolyn had no idea why Kim thought this was a good idea, but she started listing what she was grateful for that day. She started with her children, her parents, her siblings and their support, her friends, her job, Kim... Suddenly she realized that as she was talking, she could actually feel herself calming down. She began to smile as she thought of each person. Kim seemed to notice the change in Carolyn's demeanor and gave her a smile. "That didn't take long," she said. "Carolyn, it's impossible for any of us to feel stressed and blessed at the same time. Today is your lucky day. Today you get two secrets for the price of one lunch. Secret number four is that you must learn to live a life of true gratitude, and you must challenge yourself daily to see the good in your day and in your life. The big things are easy for most people to be grateful for, but it's not just the big things. The many small things that surround you daily can create a grateful heart in you."

A+ Life Secret #4

*You must learn to live a life of true gratitude
by focusing on your blessings every day.*

Kim glanced at her watch and gasped. The extra fifteen

minutes had turned into thirty minutes. Carolyn apologized to Kim and she laughed and said that she appreciated the extra-long lunch as the only thing on her schedule was working on the company budget all afternoon, which wasn't one of her favorite tasks. On the way back to the office, Kim reminded Carolyn that whenever she was feeling stressed out to remind herself of that annoying phrase, *"I'm too blessed to be stressed."*

14

Living with Gratitude

Carolyn felt completely overwhelmed as she sat down at her desk and tried to get refocused. A+ life secret number four had struck a nerve with her, and she could feel the tears start to well up again. She closed her eyes and replayed a memory of the day before Ben walked out of her life. The evening had started off fun. Ben's best friend, John, had come over. They had grilled out, had a few beers, and were enjoying time together. She couldn't recall how the conversation had started, but out of the blue John had looked her in the eye and told her she was a negative person. Her eyes filled with tears as she remembered how that had hurt her. She had tried to defend herself, but he just shook his head and laughed, and gave example after example. Ben had said nothing, nothing at all to defend her. Later, she had asked Ben why he didn't say anything, but he just shrugged and told her she was overreacting and John was probably only joking.

Carolyn had asked Ben if he thought she was a negative person, and he simply said no. Right there and then she decided that the problem was John. He was a jerk, and she didn't care if she ever saw him again. She recalled going to bed that night and wondering if others saw her as a negative person.

Carolyn had forgotten all about that evening. It had been the very next night that Ben announced he was leaving. She wiped her tears, blew her nose, and said out loud to herself, "I think John was right. I'm full of negativity, and I want it to end. Negative people are energy-drainers. I know that, and I was so busy being one that I didn't even notice I was one." Carolyn smiled and said quietly to herself, "You can't change until you own the problem, and today I'm owning it!"

Carolyn spent the rest of the afternoon trying to focus on her work, but her heart and mind kept going back to her conservation with Kim. She made a mental note to call John, mend her hurt feelings, and thank him for being honest with her, even though it hurt at the time. Carolyn looked at her watch and made an executive decision to leave work early to run to the store and pick up a new journal and something for dinner.

As she drove to the store, adrenaline ran through her. She couldn't believe how good it felt to own her problem and to make a commitment to herself to change. She was excited to start this lifework assignment, and even more excited to change her negative thinking and become a positive role model for her kids.

15

Remembering the Small Blessings

Carolyn's gratitude journaling started off easy, and she could write down 5-10 things that she was grateful for each night with no problem. By the third day, it started to feel repetitive. She was writing down the same things each day: kids, parents, siblings, friends, job. She wondered if she was doing something wrong or if something was wrong with her. She was thankful for those things, but this assignment felt a little monotonous. She decided to skip a couple of days to see if that helped, but although she could add a couple of new things, it still left her frustrated. She had tried to repeat "I'm too blessed to be stressed," but she was running into the same: simply repeating the same things over and over.

When it was time to meet with Kim, Carolyn felt embarrassed. She slowly walked out to the parking lot and got into Kim's car. Kim seemed to notice Carolyn's forced

smile, and she said, "It was harder than you thought, right?" Carolyn only nodded. On the way to the restaurant, Kim pointed out a blooming tree and talked about its beauty. She seemed overly excited about hitting all the lights just right. They walked into The Café, and Kim thanked the waitress for seating them right away. They looked at their menus and quickly ordered sandwiches, fries, and water.

As they waited for their food, Carolyn looked at Kim and said, "I feel like such a loser. Each day, I wrote the same thing down—That I was thankful for you teaching me the secrets of living an A+ life, my relationship with God, my children, parents, brothers, sister, friends, and my job. I was excited initially, and then it became boring because I kept writing down the same things. What's wrong with me?"

Kim smiled and said, "Nothing is wrong with you, Carolyn. We live in a world that focuses on the negatives. If you want to have change deep within you, you will have to dig deeper."

Carolyn looked puzzled. "What do you mean, dig deeper? I am thankful for all those things."

Kim took a deep breath and said, "Carolyn, so often we take for granted the little things in life. We forget to be thankful for the beauty around us, for the blooming of trees or flowers, for the laughter of a child playing, even just getting out of bed each morning. We forget that our sight and our hearing are blessings. Too often we forget how blessed we are that we have a roof over our head, food in the cupboards, and indoor plumbing! We forget to be thankful that someone held the door for us or gave us a

smile. Sometimes we only look for blessings in the big things and forget to focus on the little things. This week when you journal, start challenging yourself to notice the small things throughout your day and not only so you can write new things daily. By learning to see the small blessings in your life, you start to become a more positive person."

The food arrived, and before Carolyn could take her first bite, Kim said, "Carolyn, I want you to understand something. What you are learning are not just the secrets of living an A+ life, but a new way of living. To have this new way of living, you must have a new way of thinking. You must consciously think about and live these secrets daily until they simply become who you are and how you live."

Carolyn nodded in agreement and said, "They say it takes 21 days to create a new habit, so I guess I'm over half way there with the secrets."

Kim took a drink of water and said, "Carolyn, I don't know who came up with that number, but I believe it creates a false belief. I can promise you it takes longer than 21 days to be able to live and breathe these secrets without thinking much about them. This is a new way of living, and you must spend time daily on these secrets until they are just a part of who you are. For some people this takes months and for others, years."

Carolyn laughed and said, "I guess it's taken me over thirty years to become who I am today, so I better be patient while I re-train my brain!"

Kim smiled and asked Carolyn if she had been reading her life vision plan and WHY statement daily. Carolyn felt

herself turning red from embarrassment. Kim said that she understood it was hard to remember and encouraged Carolyn to make it a priority by scheduling time daily on her calendar for this life changing habit. They spent the rest of lunch discussing Carolyn's next lifework assignment. She could hardly wait to get started on her plan.

16

The Game Plan

The kids were spending the evening with Ben, and Carolyn was secretly relieved that she had an evening to herself again. She had sent Ruth a text earlier asking if she wanted to meet for dinner, but Ruth was unavailable. Carolyn decided this was a sign she was meant to eat cereal for dinner, curl up in her favorite chair with a cup of hot tea, and work on her new lifework assignment. Carolyn reflected on what Kim had shared with her that afternoon. Kim had said that to have her life vision plan come true, she would need to create a game plan. The reason so many people failed when going after their big goals and dreams was that they failed to create a genuine plan. Part of that plan should be how to stay focused on her plan. She had then gone on to quote a saying that Carolyn just loved: "A goal without a plan is just a wish." Gosh, how many times in her life had she thought she had a goal? But, her plans were always worthless because she

rarely put any energy into a plan. She couldn't remember when she had spent time reviewing her goals.

Kim had suggested that she needed to review her five-year LVP and then strategize a game plan to make it come true. Carolyn studied the areas of her LVP: health and well-being, relationships, spirituality, finances, career, personal development, physical environment/home, and fun and creativity. Kim recommended that she take each area and give it a grade, just like she did the first day they met. Now she was being asked to grade each area with the hope of accomplishing an overall GPA of A within five years. Kim had encouraged her to carefully reflect and be truthful with herself with each answer. Then, Carolyn was to create her game plan for making her current grade an A. She knew that she wanted each of the eight areas to be graded an A in the next five years, and hopefully sooner. But she knew before she could achieve this, she would have to once again be honest with herself about what grade she would currently give herself in each area.

Carolyn drew in a big breath, released it, and started to grade her life. She spent time quietly reflecting on each area and resisting the urge to give herself a better grade than she deserved. After what seemed like forever, she looked down at her "life report card" and noted that she had given herself B in health and well-being, B in relationships, C in personal development, C in fun and creativity, C in spirituality, C in finances, C in physical environment, and a B in career. Carolyn added up her score by using the GPA system she had used in high school and college, and her final GPA score

made her cringe. Her total was only a 2.37, which wasn't even a high C. She reflected back to the day Kim had asked her to grade her life and she had said C. That had been hard to swallow, but now she had each grade laid out in front of her, and it wasn't pretty. Kim had made it very clear that afternoon at lunch that if Carolyn wanted to create an A+ life, she would have to create a game plan and be willing to not only create it, but actually use it, and use it daily.

Carolyn reached over for a drink of her tea and realized that she had been so focused for the past hour, she hadn't even touched it. She took a big gulp of her now-cold tea and contemplated how to create a winning game plan. She picked up her LVP and read it over and over. She knew in her heart that she wanted it to become her reality, and she knew that she would need to create goals and timelines for her plan. Carolyn dug right in. She started by writing goals for each of her eight areas, and as she wrote, she could feel herself become energized.

Carolyn let out a sigh of relief and reviewed her work. She liked what she had done, but realized she had not completed the assignment correctly. She had left out strategizing her game plan, and had instead just rewritten her life plan in a different format. She sipped her tea as her mind raced around what she had written and how she could create a plan. Suddenly, it hit her. Both Ruth and Kim had compared her life plan to a business plan. Carolyn yelled, "BINGO!" She knew exactly how she was going create a winning game plan. Carolyn glanced at the clock and knew that she didn't have time to finish before the kids came

home, so she jotted down some notes to help her remember.

Just as she was finishing up, she heard the car pull into the driveway and the kids came running inside to give her big hugs. She gave a nod to Ben and tried to smile as he told the kids goodbye. This was always an awkward moment for her, and she guessed it was probably awkward for the kids and for Ben. She wondered how long it would take for her heart to stop aching when she saw him.

Carolyn was exhausted after getting the kids settled down from their visit with Ben. The kids seemed to be needier after these visits, and bedtime routines always took longer. She smiled as she remembered how initially that drove her crazy, but now she had moved into a preventative mindset. She would give each child extra attention on those nights, giving them a backrub, reading a story to them, or just talking to them. This seemed to make their lives a little smoother.

Carolyn crawled into her bed after the last child had his alone time with her. She felt tired, but her mind was still racing with thoughts about what should go into her master game plan. She began to feel overwhelmed by her busy schedule. She worried that she couldn't possibility have time to finish it before next Tuesday. It occurred to her that she was creating a problem that didn't need to be there in the first place. She told Lucy to get out of her head, and then she told herself that she would work on one section of her master game plan each evening after the kids went to bed. Carolyn pulled out her life vision plan and her WHY statement to read one more time before she went to sleep.

This seemed to quiet her restless thoughts, and she quickly fell asleep.

17

Strategy Through Daily Action

Carolyn hadn't felt this energized in a long time. She was so proud of her game plan and couldn't wait to share it with Kim. She had worked a little bit each night to create a plan that she would commit to 100% for the long run. Carolyn pulled into the parking lot where she was meeting Kim for lunch. She laughed to herself as she thought about the previous weeks and how she had almost quit. She was so thankful that she had stayed committed to the process and couldn't wait to learn the next secret. Kim pulled into the parking spot next to her, and they walked into West Street Deli together. The difference all this was making was written on Carolyn's face and even in the way she walked. Kim told her this was the part she always enjoyed. She had taught the secrets to five other women, and so far, no one had quit. They were all living A+ lives!

Carolyn couldn't wait to start sharing, so she quickly

ordered a tuna sandwich on sourdough bread with Swiss cheese and a side salad. The server brought over their drinks as she pulled her master plan out of her purse. She shared with Kim how she had graded each area of her life and planned out where she wanted to be in five years. She laughed and shared that her overall life grade point average was a low C. She had started with her vision of what she wanted her life to look like in five years and then created her plan by working backward. She went into detail about what she wanted to accomplish each year to create this amazing life. Kim was impressed with all the detail and thought put into her plan. But her next question threw Carolyn off. "Carolyn, this plan is great, but what are you going to start doing today to make it your reality?"

Carolyn sat quietly reflecting on this question. At work, the business plan was always a team effort, and the team helped to hold people accountable, but this was different. There was no team, only her. Carolyn was stumped and looked to Kim for help. Kim told her this part was difficult for most people. "Carolyn, let me give you some advice that my mentor gave me years ago. Your year-to-year plan looks great, but a year can be overwhelming. The missing piece is that you must break down your first year into what needs to be done every month. Once you have figured out what needs to be done every month, you must look at the first month and break it down into weeks."

Carolyn laughed and said, "Okay, okay, I think I get it. Once I've broken it down into weeks, I then must break it into days, and that is how I create little action steps daily to

create my amazing A+ life!"

Kim smiled and told Carolyn she got an A+ on this assignment. Kim went on to suggest to Carolyn that most people struggle with breaking down a year, and she suggested that Carolyn break her year down into three-month increments which would be easier to grasp and evaluate.

As they were walking out to the parking lot, Carolyn looked at Kim and said, "You haven't said anything about my plan to leave the company within five years to start my own business. Are you mad?"

Kim stopped and said, "In all honesty, I have mixed emotions. You're a wonderful asset to the company, but it would be selfish of me to say that I want you to stay. Those who are not living their dreams all-too-often become unhappy people, not only at home but also at work, and unhappy people at work don't create a fun culture."

Carolyn hadn't realized she had been holding her breath while Kim was talking. She let out a sigh that surprised them both. Kim smiled and said, "Remember, to make your LVP come to life, you must have a strategy for success and a game plan that works for you. Your game plan looks at your long-range plan and then breaks it down into years, months, weeks, then days. Each day you must work on your plan by creating action steps that bring you closer to your amazing future!"

A+ Secret #5

You must have a strategy for success and a game plan broken down into daily action steps that work for you.

Kim gave Carolyn a big hug and said, "Always remember that it's the little things you do each day that help you create your amazing future. To ensure success, you must create daily action steps that get you one day closer to your vision." Carolyn returned the hug and said, "Wait a minute. I'm already past my lunch hour, and you haven't shared the last secret." Carolyn could feel herself getting anxious. She had an appointment back in the office in less than thirty minutes.

Kim laughed and said, "I almost forgot to tell you. This week is all about practicing and living all that you've learned. Have you ever heard the saying that it takes 10,000 hours to become an expert?" Carolyn shook her head. Kim grinned. "They say that it takes 10,000 hours to become an expert at something, so for you to become an expert on you and how you want to live, you must believe that it is possible and you must practice this new awareness and this new of way of living."

Carolyn nodded and said, "My mom always said, 'practice makes perfect.'"

Kim nodded. "This week, your lifework assignment is to practice everything that you have learned and implement it fully into your life."

On the way back to the office, Carolyn couldn't help but smile thinking about becoming an expert on her life and how it was going to look so amazing on her journey to 10,000 hours.

18

The Secret that Pulls It All Together

Earlier in the week, Kim had asked Carolyn if she could take her out to dinner to share the last secret and celebrate her success in sticking around to hear them all. This time they scheduled for Friday night. The extra three days of waiting were driving Carolyn crazy. She was excited to hear the last of the secrets. Friday evening finally came, and as Carolyn drove, she kept contemplating what the last secret could be. She just couldn't figure out what was still missing. She pulled into the parking lot and noticed that Kim's car was already there. She glanced at the clock to make sure she wasn't late and was relieved to see that she was still five minutes early. Carolyn walked into Ge-Angelo's and smelled the aroma of Italian food. This restaurant made the best lasagna in town, and she couldn't wait to order that with her favorite red wine. Carolyn spotted Kim waiting in the back

of the waiting room and walked over to greet her.

Kim had already put her name in, so it didn't take long for them to be seated. She told Carolyn, "I can't believe that we've already gone through the first five secrets and now it's time for me to share the last secret, the secret that pulls it all together. Before we get started, let's order a big glass of wine and some dinner." While they waited for their wine, Kim asked Carolyn about the previous week; if she was following through with practicing and living with this new mindset. Carolyn admitted that at times it was hard. On a few occasions, she found herself completely forgetting everything she had learned and heard herself being whiny and negative. Kim thanked her for her honesty and said, "Remember, you can't change what you don't take ownership of and that includes your thoughts and actions." Carolyn nodded, liking the new motto Kim had taught her.

Their wine came, and after they had enjoyed a few sips, Kim looked Carolyn square in the eye and said, "Carolyn, the real secret is that for this all to work, you must believe deep down within you that it can happen. You must believe that you are worthy of this amazing future and that you can create it." Carolyn shook her head. She believed every word Kim had said, but she could hear Lucy saying she set the bar too high to truly believe. Kim continued, "To make it come alive, you must know your plan inside and out. You must also know your WHY statement for those days when you want to throw the in towel and let Lucy win." Carolyn smiled and wondered if Kim knew that she was struggling to believe.

Kim took Carolyn's hand and said, "I know this is all a

little overwhelming, but I know you can do it. Remember that I want you to read your vision plan every day, and if you are struggling, read it two or three times a day." Kim went on to suggest that Carolyn modify parts of her vision by adding the simple words, "I'm willing," to her plan. Kim explained that it was a simple a mind trick, "Our brain believes whatever we 'feed' it. If we tell our brains that we are willing to find financial success, our brains will help us find that success. Therefore, if we tell our brains we are tired of being financially strained, our brains will look for proof that we are financially strained. That is why it is so important to 'feed' your brain positivity." Kim looked at Carolyn and asked her if she had ever heard the statement "fake it until you make it." Carolyn nodded. "There is truth behind that statement. Your brain doesn't know the difference between truth and reality. It only knows what you feed it. So my advice is to feed it well."

Carolyn felt her head spinning, and she knew that it wasn't because of the wine. It seemed like Kim kept adding more and more rules to her vision. Kim asked her to share what she was thinking. Carolyn gave a heavy sigh and said, "I've already made my plan and this seems like a plan on top of my plan."

Kim nodded and said, "You are exactly right, but even the best laid plans can go astray. What I'm asking you to do is to make your dream your new reality, and to do that you must strategize for success. You have a game plan, but what are you going to do when you have a setback, challenges, or obstacles along your journey? Let me give you an example

to help you understand. Last year, my good friend went on a cruise and was very excited. In anticipation of the vacation, she created a goal to lose weight by exercising and eating right. A few weeks before the cruise, she called me in a panic. She had lost the desired weight and was pleased with herself, but she was panicking because she knew she would be able to eat whenever and whatever on her seven-day cruise."

Carolyn wondered where this was going, but she continued to listen. "Carolyn, what my friend forgot was that she needed to create a plan for success on her vacation. She needed to first remember her WHY regarding her health vision, and that her weight loss wasn't just about looking good for her vacation. It was about a healthier lifestyle. She was fortunate because she could plan for her obstacle. Most of the time our obstacles just show up out of nowhere, like a roadblock. You think you are going along just fine when suddenly, BAM, you must redirect. I can't say this enough, Carolyn. This is the reason your WHY is so important. You will run into your own roadblocks on your life journey; we all do. I want you to be prepared. This last secret pulls it all together, and in a way, it's many secrets. You must first and foremost make time to regularly review your plan and make adjustments as needed. Next, I know that I have already said this, but you must know your WHY inside and out so that you can be fully prepared when roadblocks pop up. All too often these roadblocks throw people so far off course that they quit. But, when you know your WHY, you can re-focus and get back on track. Lastly, you must believe with all your heart and mind that your LVP is possible."

A+ Secret #6

Your LVP is a work in progress, and you must schedule regular review times. As you review, you must believe with all your mind and heart that your vision will become your new reality.

As Kim was paying the waitress, Carolyn asked a question that had been weighing on her mind. "Kim, this is all wonderful, and I know in the short run I won't forget a thing, but how do I remember it a year from now? How do I keep this my focus, or should I say, how do I keep myself accountable to my own plan?"

Kim smiled. "Carolyn, this can be part of your plan. If you are struggling to remember, then you need to schedule more meetings with yourself to review your plan. If you still find yourself struggling and you hear yourself listening to and believing your excuses, then it is time for you to find an accountability partner. Better yet, hire a coach trained to help you identify your excuses along with your Stinkin' Thinkin' errors. What's important to remember is that only you can make this work, which means you must do the work."

The Extra Secret

Carolyn couldn't believe it. It had been over seven years since her first meeting with Kim, and her life had improved every year. To celebrate, Carolyn had planned a trip to the Caribbean with her family. She pulled out her suitcase to begin packing when she suddenly sat down on the edge of her bed, feeling overwhelmed with joy. Cooper walked over, put his arm around her, and asked, "Honey, what's the matter?"

Carolyn looked up and gave him a tight hug. "Absolutely nothing is the matter, Cooper, I just feel so blessed." She squeezed his hand. "Over seven years ago, my life crashed down around me. Then, I met Kim and learned the six secrets of living an A+ life. Now everything in my life is better than I could have ever imagined."

Cooper smiled at her. He knew her success story well. Carolyn continued, "By creating my life vision plan,

understanding my WHY, and learning to live with Lucy, my
life has completely changed. I've met you. We have a
wonderful relationship with each other and with our children.
My faith has never been stronger. Last year, I created my very
own dream job!" Carolyn shook her head. At times it was still
hard to wrap her head around it. She laughed, thinking about
the last seven years. There had been times she had wanted to
quit, and she was thankful that Kim had made her drill her
WHY statement into her head. She reflected on the day Kim
had talked about living an A+ life. Back then, Carolyn
thought living an A+ life meant having it all: the money,
house, car, vacations, clothing... she was so confused back
then, thinking all that would equal living a perfect life. She
now understood that this wasn't at all true and that none of
those things could bring her the joy that now filled her. She
still had difficult times, but she handled them differently. The
difficult times didn't consume her or go on and on because
she had a strong foundation to help center her. Her habit of
starting her day with gratitude had helped her get control of
Lucy's negative thinking. She could see how this simple
change had impacted many areas of her life, but especially
her relationship with her children.

Carolyn loved sharing the secrets of living an A+ life
with others and had already mentored eight women who at
the time were going through various life changes: divorce,
mid-life crises, retirement, relationship issues. She loved
watching how the secrets impacted their lives, but she felt
something was missing in her approach. She wondered if she
could impact someone's life before a crisis. She wondered if

she could help someone think differently to live differently.

Carolyn believed that each person is born with a purpose, and that purpose is often disguised as a big dream in a person's heart. She had come to realize that there are five kinds of people. The first type has a dream, but doesn't know that they can act on their dreams so they brush off their dream as foolish thinking. The second type is the person who knows she has a big dream in her heart, but blames life's circumstances for why it can never come true. The third type of person lets fear stop them from ever going after their big dream. Some might fear failure, while others might fear success. They fear what others will think, they fear rejection, they fear getting out of their comfort zone, and they let fear stop them from accomplishing their dream. The fourth type declares that their life is just too busy to go after their big dream. They are the time-blamer, justifying that someday they will go after their big dream when the kids start school, when finances get better, when they have enough money in the bank, or when the kids leave home. They always put it off, and when the circumstances are finally in alignment, they declare that they are now too old to go after their big dream. The last type knows in their heart that they have been given a dream, and they strategize for success, not allowing their fear or excuses to get in the way. It had taken Carolyn five years to figure out what she wanted to do with her life and to take the leap. She had become a coach, which had also led her to become a professional speaker. Carolyn knew with all her heart that everyone had the potential to live the life of their dreams, if they were willing to hold true to the secrets.

After living with the six secrets for seven years, Carolyn had come to believe that the six secrets needed one more secret. Carolyn had taken everything Kim had taught her and come to understand the importance of living her life in alignment with her priorities. She now understood that a balanced life doesn't mean that you spend equal time in all areas of your life. A balanced life is when you are living in alignment with your priorities. Carolyn practiced this daily by scheduling time on her calendar for her top four priorities: growing her faith, family time, taking care of her health, and then focusing on her career. She loved her early morning routine of getting up early for quiet devotion and time with God, having coffee with Cooper, and exercising, all before the kids got up. By the time their alarms went off, she was ready for mom time without feeling stressed out. The simple act of scheduling her priorities had changed her chaotic life to a life of joy and peace.

A+ Secret #7

When you are living your life in alignment with your priorities, you will find your greatest sense of joy and peace.

Carolyn closed her suitcase and moved it off the bed. She glanced at the clock and knew she needed to get to bed and go to sleep fast, as they had an early morning flight to catch. As she crawled into bed, she thanked God for Kim coming into her life, sharing the secrets with her, and changing her life forever. As she pulled up the covers, she

said her nightly prayer: that God would use her again to help others find the joy and peace that they desired in their lives.

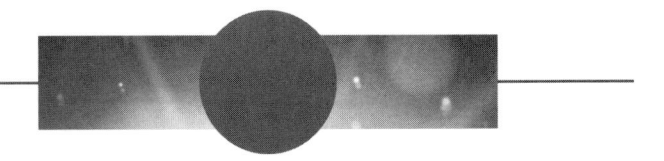

7-Secrets of Living an A+ Life

1. Before you can start living an A+ life, you must first visualize what your A+ life looks like.

2. Your WHY statement is your secret weapon to help you stay focused, even when you want to give up.

3. You must learn how to master your mindset and turn your Inner Bully into your Inner Cheerleader.

4. You must learn to live a life of true gratitude by focusing on your blessings every day.

5. You must have a strategy for success and a game plan broken down into daily action steps that work for you.

6. Your LVP is a work in progress, and you must schedule regular review times. As you review, you must believe with all your mind and heart that your vision will become your new reality.

7. When you are living your life in alignment with your
   priorities, you will find your greatest sense of joy
   and peace.

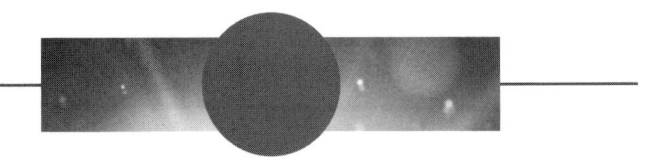

Finding Your Joy Action Plan

The 7-Secrets of Living an A+ Life Action Plan was developed to empower you to create the life, business, organization, or family that you have been dreaming about. If you are tired of dreaming, if you are tired of wishing, if you are tired of complaining, then it's time for you to start Step 1. Are you ready?

Step 1: Create a life vision plan (LVP) of what success looks like to you.

Begin this journey by writing down what you would like your life to look like in the next five-plus years. It's important during this process to dream BIG and to not shy away from this challenge. To help you get started, you can spend some time reflecting on these questions:

- What do I want to accomplish both personally and professionally?

- What is most important to me?

- What are my values?

- What do I want my most important relationships to look like?

- How do I want to spend my free time?

- If I knew I couldn't fail, what would I be doing?

- What income do I desire?

- In what areas do I want to grow or learn?

- What is on my bucket list that I would like to complete?

- The time to start creating my legacy is NOW. What legacy do I want to leave?

Questions to ask your business or organization:

- What do we hope to accomplish?

- What is our main purpose?

- In five years, ten years, etc. …what do we want our company to look like?

- How does our business or organization benefit others?

- What do we want our ideal clients saying about us?

Step 2: Create your WHY statement.

Your WHY statement is going to help you stay focused even when you want to give up. It is your secret weapon to finding the success you desire. Discovering your WHY is like peeling an onion. Don't settle for your first answer. Dig deep until you reach your core WHY. This will help drive you on days when you want to give up.

In order to remember your WHY statement, you must have it written down throughout your home and workplace. A good strategy is to place it in an area where you sometimes feel weak. Read it often. Know it like the back of your hand. Your WHY should resonate throughout your whole being. Your WHY is your secret weapon for success. Why is it important for your life vision plan to become your reality? Why is your goal important? When you answer your first WHY, it's important to realize that it's not your inner most WHY. Continue to dig deeper and ask yourself the question over and over until you've reached your deepest core WHY.

Step 3: Master your mindset.

You must learn how to master your mindset and turn your Inner Bully into your Inner Cheerleader.

Eleven symptoms that show you may be struggling with Stinkin' Thinkin':

1. Perfectionist: This bully expects you to do

everything perfectly and makes it difficult for you to accept your work or yourself without criticism. She can cause problems at work and at home, as nothing is ever good enough.

2. **Scarcity Thoughts:** This bully lets you think that things are never going to get better. She wants you to think that you will never have enough knowledge, money, resources, or time.

3. **Blaming the Past:** You might be struggling with this bully if you hear yourself say, "I've been down this road before and it didn't work out, so why even go there?" This bully keeps you stuck in the past so you can't have the future you want.

4. **Being Defensive:** This bully likes to jump to the conclusion that someone is judging her or thinking the worst of her. She has a tone in her voice of: "What do you mean?"

5. **Taking Things Personally:** This bully likes to twist things around to make her feel sorry for herself. She typically feels like people are intentionally wronging her, and she will often give up on goals or relationships, feeling it is someone or something else's fault.

6. **Comparing Self to Others:** This bully compares herself to her peers in all areas of her life. She

judges your home, income, clothing, children, etc. —always against others.

7. **Victim Mindset:** This bully is like the Taking Things Personally bully, but goes a step further. If you hear yourself blaming others instead of looking at yourself, you may struggle with Victim Mindset.

8. **Excuses:** This bully is rampant in most people's minds. She always has her finger pointing at someone or something else. "It's not my fault I didn't get the paper turned in; the internet went down." "It's not my fault I didn't exercise this week; the weather was too cold." "It's not my fault dinner isn't ready; my mom called."

9. **Name Caller:** This bully is a mean one who turns to name calling when frustrated or unhappy. "You are so stupid!" "You look like a fat pig in those jeans!" "I can't believe that you can't figure out this computer problem again; you're such an idiot!"

10. **Complainer:** This bully struggles to take ownership and often sounds whiny. "It's the teacher's fault; she only gave us enough time to complete one assignment." "I did my part; it's not my fault the team didn't follow through."

11. **Ignorer:** This bully deflects problems by becoming the jokester or by burying her head in the sand and ignoring the issue altogether.

It's important to know that everyone has Stinkin' Thinkin' in their head, but you can't fix a problem that you don't own. Before you can master your mindset, you must first acknowledge what Stinkin' Thinkin' errors your Inner Bully is throwing at you. Don't be surprised to find that you have several areas that could use some work. Changing our thinking takes time and practice, so pick two to three Stinkin' Thinkin' errors to zero in on. When you hear yourself using one of the identified thinking errors, simply stop and correct your thinking. If you would like extra accountability, share the Stinkin' Thinkin' errors you are working on with an accountability partner, and let the fun begin.

Step 4: Live a life of gratitude.

The world is full of negativity, and if you're not careful, you can be sucked into that train of thought. Living a life of gratitude is a lifestyle change, and it requires time and practice. What you feed your mind, you believe, so it's important to start each new day with thoughts of gratitude. Challenge yourself to dig deep each day to see the blessings in your life. The more you practice this new mindset, the more you will deepen your sense of gratitude. It's important not to brush this step off. It's easy to do. Remember, the world is full of negativity, which impacts you and your thoughts.

Step 5: Create a game plan.

Before you can create success, you must know what it means to you. Be careful not to just accept what the world calls successful. Money, fame, fancy homes, and fancy cars may bring you material happiness, but it can cost you in other areas such as your health, relationships, fun, and creativity. To create an A+ life, you must first strategize what an A+ life looks like in all areas. To help you better understand this, take the Life GPA assessment to help you create a game plan for your life.

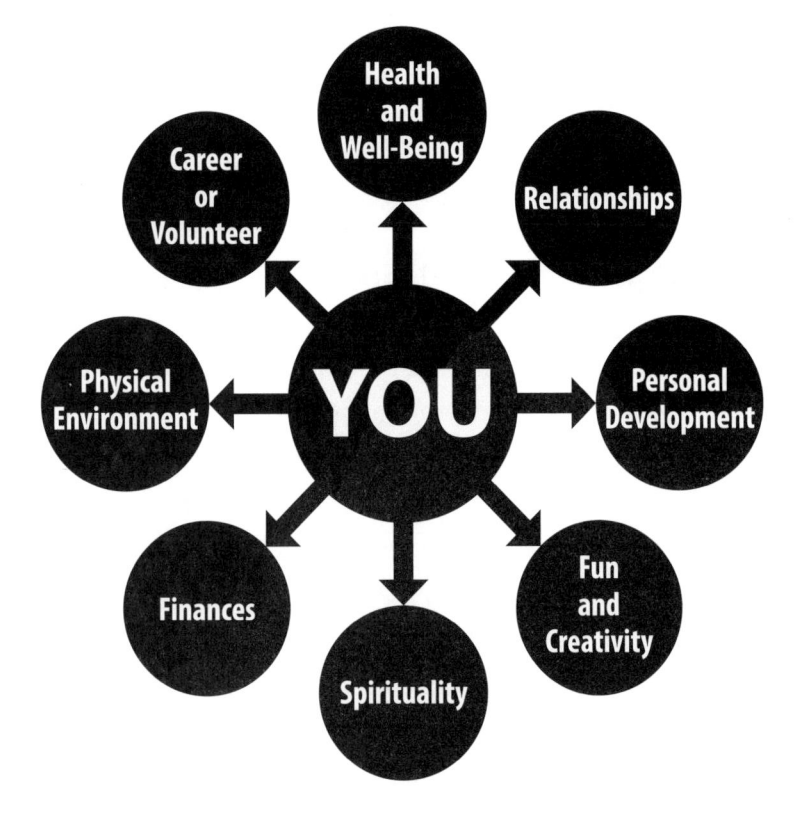

Life GPA Assessment

GRADE	DESCRIPTION	SCORE
A	Awesome	4
B	Better than Average	3
C	Average	2
D	Down in the Dumps	1
F	Flunking	0

Life GPA score

Overall GPA score_____

Read the brief description of each circle (see below) and decide what letter grade to give that area of your life for the past quarter. If a particular area doesn't currently resonate with you, feel free not to address it at this time. Once you have graded yourself in all areas, add up your total and divide by the number of grades. This will calculate your current life grade.

It's important to note that everyone goes through life with ups and downs. When we are mindful of that fact and have a plan for our D and F times, we can get through those times more easily and hopefully more quickly as we are

living our lives with intention and focus.

Health and Well-Being: Are you happy with your physical and mental health? Weight? Overall health? Level of stress?

Relationships: It might be easier to break your most significant relationships down into different areas such as: significant other, children, extended family, friendships, etc. Ask yourself how you would like to see those relationships grow. In five-plus years, what do you hope those relationships will look like? Do you enjoy spending time with the people in your current relationships? Do you have toxic relationships that are robbing you of joy? What would make your relationships more joyful?

Personal Development: This typically covers areas of growth and learning that you would like to see. It could tie in with other areas such as finances, spirituality, health, and wellness. Ask yourself: Do I spend enough time growing and developing in areas that I am interested in?

Fun and Creativity: All too often our fun time gets wrapped up in business events or kids' events. Those activities can still be fun, but sometimes we forget that we once enjoyed things outside of work and kids. Do you feel that you are getting enough fun and creativity time in your life? Are there fun parts of your life that are always getting put on the back burner because of how busy you are?

Spirituality: Do you feel that your journey of growing and maturing in your faith and/or beliefs is getting the attention that it deserves? Do you ever wish that you felt more connected?

Finances: Your score around finances can relate to your current income, expenses, debt, savings, or where you would like to see yourself in the future. Ask yourself: Am I currently satisfied with my income? Am I spending too much? Do I feel that I am saving enough money from each paycheck? Are my income and spending habits helping or hurting my five-year vision for my life?

Physical Environment: This area typically centers around your home or office. Ask yourself: Are you satisfied with the community in which you live and work? Do you enjoy your neighborhood? Do you want to make changes to your home, such as painting, flooring, etc...? What changes would you need to make to create your five-year vision?

Career or Volunteer Experience: Ask yourself: How satisfied am I at my current position? What would need to change to make this a better experience? Do I want to be doing this in five-plus years? What do I need to do differently to bring more joy to this area of my life?

Remember, to create your own personalized game plan, you must first know what you are shooting for to find the success you desire.

Step 6: Strategize, Review, and Believe

Your life plan is a work in progress, and you must set aside time every three months to review and strategize your plan. It's okay to tweak or modify your plan as you start to live it. If you are struggling with your plan, take time to

---

My WHY:

My Goal is:

I will do this by: LIST DATE_____ TIME_____

I will commit to make these **daily changes** to my time and schedule:

I will commit to make these **weekly changes** to my time and schedule:

I will commit to make these **lifestyle changes**:

Financial Investments:

I will commit to put aside _____ to realize my goals tomorrow.

Tracking:

I will use this tracking method to track my progress: _____

Accountability:

My accountability partner is_____

I will have an accountability check every_____

I will schedule quarterly meetings to review and update my LVP, goals, and action steps. Next quarterly check-in: _____

Long term success looks like:

---

reflect on your WHY. Most importantly, as you review, you must believe with all your mind and heart that your big dreams will become your new reality.

Step 7: Live in alignment with your priorities.

Ask yourself: if someone were to look at your expenses or calendar, what would they say your priorities are? Your priorities are typically people or things in your life that are part of your foundation. Once you know what your priorities are, take time to schedule them first on your calendar each week. First means before anything is placed on your calendar. When you are living your life in alignment with your priorities, you will find your greatest sense of joy and peace.

Carrie Copley is a success coach, speaker, trainer, and author. Carrie's purpose is to empower others to create the life and business they dream of living.

Visit my website, www.loveyourlife2.com:

- To download the Finding Joy Action Plan.

- To learn more about launching this new initiative at your company or organization.

- For assistance with turning around low-energy teams or relationships.

- To discover how to enhance morale, productivity, and performance.

- To learn more about Carrie and how to work with her for individual or group coaching.

To learn more please contact Love Your Life, LLC at:

Carrie@loveyourlife2.com
www.loveyourlife2.com
(515)-291-4380